Martin Leman's
CONTENTED
CATS

Pelham Books

W9-CEI-855

Sometimes when I have racked my brain

In writing sonnet or quartrain,

My Cat lies curled up like a ball,

Asleep, oblivious to it all.

And then perhaps at last when I

Achieve my aim, and breathe a sigh

Of gratitude, she wakes and views

Me wonderingly, as if the muse

Were something she would hardly deem

As worthwhile, say – as meat or cream,

And languidly she eyes my sonnet,

Then stretches and sits down upon it.

Margaret E. Bruner · Muse versus mews

Christmas '91

This book belongs to

Dianne Vultaggio

May you and your cats always
be content.
We look forward to visiting
Lady Di, Queen Grey and
Princess Sheena at their new
residence Springvale Manor.
All our love, Karen & Stephen

Scruffty on quilt

*W*ould you care for me, as I care for my cat?

Oh, I know she is treacherous

And her thoughts go no higher

Than mice and milk

And a place by my fire;

She's getting old and fat.

But when I sit alone in my evening chair,

I stroke her fur –

I like to know she is there

And to hear her purr. –

Of course, you could not care for me

Like that!

I can not purr as flatteringly

As a cat.

Anon · Plea for a cat

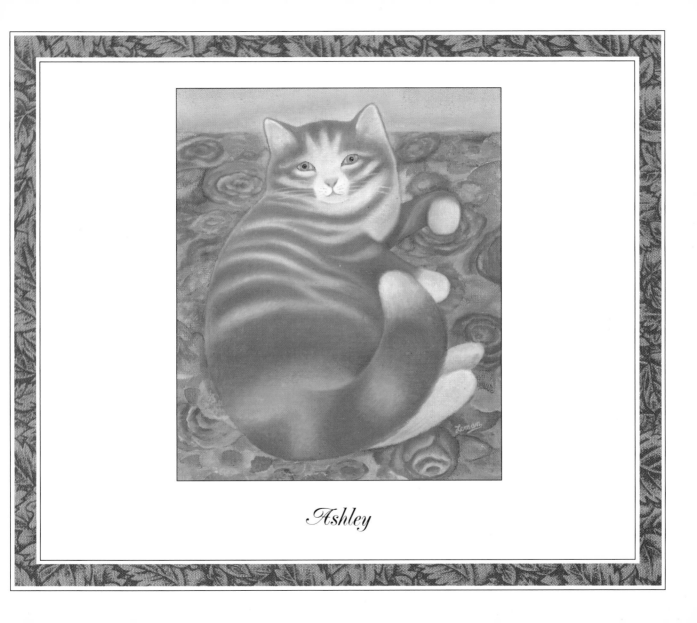

Ashley

When Dulcie lived in Carson Close

No mouse would dare to show its nose.

On her approach each rat and mole

Would promptly scurry down its hole.

The birds when flying overhead

Knew if they landed, they were dead!

They said this nonsense soon must cease

Then we can have a little peace.

But round the garden night a day

Brave Dulcie prowled and killed her prey.

For them a great catastrophy,

But Dulcie gained her Ph D.

Kit and Arthur Law · How Dulciana obtained
her Doctorate in Mouseology

Boswell & Johnson

When Tabby crouches by the fire,
Primly agaze, her eyes are rings
Of agate flame: and strange desire
Burns there, and old unholy things.

Surges on dream the lost Delight:
And off she goes, careering down
The windy archways of the night,
Afar on flying broomsticks blown.

R.W.D. Fuller · The Familiar

Swee'pea

Always well-behaved am I,

Never scratch and never cry;

Only touch the diner's hand,

So that he can understand

That I want a modest share

Of the good things that are there.

If he pay but scanty heed

To my little stomach's need,

I beg him with a mew polite

To give me just a single bite.

Greedy though that diner be,

He will share his meal with me.

Antoinette Deshoulieres · Politeness Counts

Goldie

*O*ur old cat has kittens three,
And what do you think their names shall be?
Pepper-pot, Sootikins, Scratch-away, – there!
Was there ever a kitten with these to compare?
And we call their old mother, – now, what do you think?
Tabitha Long-Claws Tiddley-Wink!

Thomas Hood · Tabitha Long-Claws Tiddley-Wink

Tosca, Tatiana and Mimi

$\mathcal{L}$et take a cat, and foster hire with milke

And Tendre flesh, and make hire couche of silke,

And let hire see a mous go by the wall,

Anon she wieveth milke and flesh, and all,

And every deintee that is in the hous,

Swiche appetit hath she to ete the mous.

Geoffrey Chaucer · The Manciple's Tale

Rosie

Hearths are quite the favourite place
For cats to slip into good grace:
They stretch where flames high-light their fur,
Tuning the room with soothing purr.
At charming they are extra smart,
Knowing sly wiles to win one's heart.

Undoubtedly the prudent cat
Is nature's choicest diplomat.

Lee Richard Hayman · Feline Fetchery

New Moon

Saint Jerome in his study kept a great big cat,

It's always in his pictures, with its feet upon the mat.

Did he give it milk to drink, in a little dish?

When it came to Fridays, did he give it fish?

If I lost my little cat, I'd be sad without it;

I should ask Saint Jeremy what to do about it;

I should ask Saint Jeremy, just because of that,

For he's the only saint I know who kept a pussy cat.

Anon · Saint Jerome and his cat

Tabby

$\mathcal{L}$ady, when you rub your face
In private room or public place,
Or reprimand each curl that strays
With tactful pat,
See that you do it with the grace
Of Tib, my cat.

Oliver St. John Gogarty · Lady – Please!

White Christmas

I'll tell you a tale of two Siamese,

They're brave and courageous and bold as you please!

They once stalked a pigeon,

This terrible pair,

And when it flew off they faked not to care.

They pretended to be on a leisurely walk,

Not out and about on a mad hunting stalk.

This duo of mine

Think they are fine,

Sitting so proudly

And mewing so loudly.

At night they just cuddle together,

Shutting out the world, what ever the weather.

Gabrielle Drake · The Two Siamese

Moët and Chandon

The Cat's a four-legged Quadruped –
Not countin' in his tail,
The Mrs. is the Tabby Cat
And Thomas is the male.

The Cat it is carnivorous,
Although to milk inclinin',
It makes a hump out of its back,
And whiskers it looks fine in.

No home should be without the Cat,
Aspeshly where there's Mouses.
It never goes away, the Cat,
But stays jest where the house is.

Anthony Euwer · The Cat

Boris

When kittens nap in pansy beds
And drowse the sunny hours,
I can't tell which are spotted cats
And which are spotted flowers!

Beryl Swift · Confusion

Cara

Taffy, the topaz-coloured cat,
Thinks now of this and now of that,
But chiefly of his meals.
Asparagus, and cream, and fish,
Are objects of his Freudian wish;
What you don't give, he steals.

His amiable amber eyes
Are very friendly, very wise;
Like Buddha, grave and fat,
He sits, regardless of applause,
And thinking, as he kneads his paws,
What fun to be a cat!

Christopher Morley · In Honour of Taffy Topaz

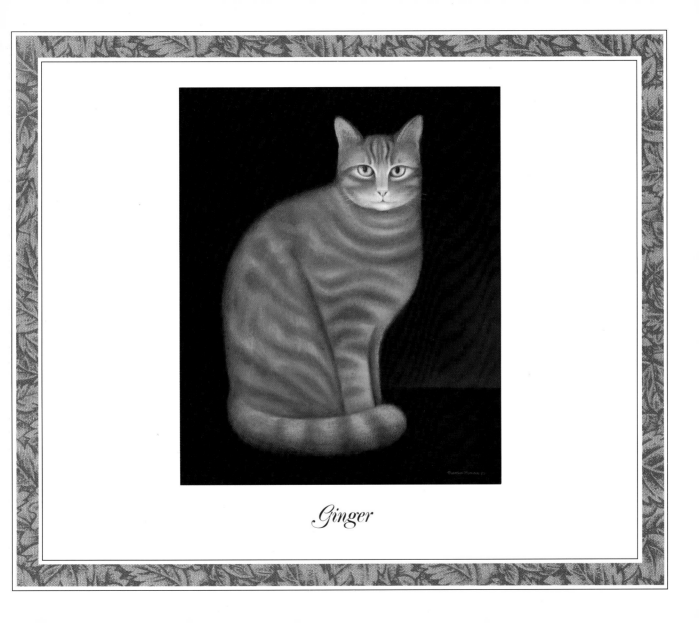

Ginger

She owns a back-yard garden with one tree,

Where she parades as though it were a park.

She takes small time for satined luxury,

Her duties wait, below-stairs, after dark.

Under a late moon, sometimes we have seen

Her coming out, triumphant, with her mouse

While, from a wall, her would-be confreres lean

With caterwauled impatience for carouse.

But she has lived her span of years apart,

Chaste and decorous; coat immaculate;

Taking her tone of conduct from the heart

Of ancient mistresses who dwell in state.

Jerusha, with gold-eyed nocturnal skill

Who bounds a garden with a jungle, still!

Edna Mead · Jerusha

Tiger Lily, Bluebell, Guinness and Marigold

Bathsheba:

    To whom none ever said scat,

    No worthier cat

    Ever sat on a mat

    Or caught a rat:

        Requies-cat.

John Greenleaf Whittier · Epitaph

Abigail

Hear our prayer, Lord, for all animals,
May they be well-fed and well-treated and happy:
Protect them from hunger and fear and suffering:
And, we pray, protect specially, dear Lord,
The little Cat who is the companion of our home,
Keep her safe as she goes abroad,
And bring her back to comfort us.

Anon · An old Russian prayer

Sears and Roebuck

Careful observers may foretell the hour
(By sure prognostics) when to dread a shower;
While rain depends, the pensive cat gives o'er
Her frolics, and pursues her tail no more.

Jonathan Swift · The cat and the rain

Gilda

T am the cat of cats. I am
The everlasting cat!
Cunning, and old, and sleek as jam,
The everlasting cat!
I hunt the vermin in the night –
The everlasting cat!
For I see best without the light –
The everlasting cat!

Anon · The Cat of Cats

Nancy's Cat

For some time we have been collecting a variety of writings on the subject of cats and should like to thank all those people who have sent us copies of poems and prose that they have enjoyed. We should like to express our gratitude here and apologise to any owners of copyright which we have been unable to trace.

Martin Leman would like to thank all those who either commissioned or allowed him to paint their cats. Special thanks to Sue Johnson Newall, Sue Pease, Louise and Paul Drake, Sally and Andrew Grad, Nancy Webber, Henrietta and Paul Garside, Natalie Gibson, Tim Wheeler and Deborah Ashforth, Margaret and Iain Coates, and Wendy and Robin Jacobs.

PELHAM BOOKS

Published by the Penguin Group
27 Wrights Lane, London W8 5TZ, England
Viking Penguin Inc., 375 Hudson Street, New York, New York 10014, USA
Penguin Books Australia Ltd, Ringwood, Victoria, Australia
Penguin Books Canada Ltd, 10 Alcorn Avenue, Toronto, Ontario, Canada M4V 3B2
Penguin Books (NZ) Ltd, 182-190 Wairau Road, Auckland 10, New Zealand

Penguin Books Ltd, Registered Offices: Harmondsworth, Middlesex, England

First published 1991

Copyright © Jill and Martin Leman 1991

Research and design by Jill Leman

Typeset by Pastiche, London
Colour origination by Anglia Graphics, Bedford
Printed and bound in Italy by L.E.G.O.

A CIP catalogue for this book is available from the British Library
Library of Congress Catalog Number 91 61347

ISBN 0 7207 2002 8